Cage Your Rage Leader's Guide

by

Murray C. Cullen and Ronald R. Cullen

Copyright 1997 by The American Correctional Association

Reginald Wilkinson, President
James A. Gondles, Jr., Executive Director
Gabriella M. Daley, Director, Communications and Publications
Leslie A. Maxam, Assistant Director, Communications and Publications
Alice Fins, Managing Editor
Michael Kelly, Associate Editor
Mike Selby, Production Editor

Printed in the United States of America by Graphic Communications, Inc., Upper Marlboro, MD.

The reproduction, distribution or inclusion in other publications of materials in this book is prohibited without prior written permission from the American Correctional Association. Note: Facilitators may reproduce the Anger Checklist Sheet #1 and #2, the Role Play Development Sheet, the Postrole Play Group Questions and Discussion Sheet, the Role Play Checklist and Probing Questions; the Feedback Sheet; and the Evaluation Form.

ISBN 1-56991-058-8

This publication may be ordered from:
The American Correctional Association
4380 Forbes Boulevard
Lanham, MD 20706-4322
1-800-ACA-JOIN

Dedication and Acknowledgments
This manual is dedicated to our sister, Anna, and Chris and John, the next generation of "Cullen/Brother authors."

Foreword

This trainer's manual enables those delivering anger-management programs to do so with greater ease and skill than they might otherwise be able to do. It allows both the trained leader and the inexperienced facilitator to deliver this proven program.

The Cage Your Rage program has been used successfully in prisons, jails, halfway houses, community facilities and other sites. Besides this manual, there are the *Cage Your Rage* workbooks and a video program. Because the original Cage Your Rage program was so successful, we developed *Cage Your Rage for Teens* and recommended this to those who work with adolescents.

This manual anticipates the type of obstacles that many leaders may encounter and provides suggestions that will enable the program to run smoothly. We believe anger management programs and other preventive programs can make a difference and lower the amount of crime and violence in our society. We wish the leaders and the participants in these programs the best in completing these activities and in living their lives with less aggression and more joy.

James A. Gondles, Jr.
Executive Director, American Correctional Association

Introduction

"Facilitator" is a generic term that refers to those who lead discussions and direct individuals and groups in dealing with their anger. This manual is an attempt to present ideas and activities to provide a base to help support any anger management program, especially the *Cage Your Rage* program by Murray Cullen.

This manual is suitable for those working with both males and females in correctional facilities, court-ordered probation or parole-directed treatment, or other types of community programs. Those who may profitably use this manual include: probation and parole officials; living-skills coaches; correctional programming staff; social service agency workers; and members of community groups, family shelters, hospitals, and public health agencies.

Many of the ideas and examples presented in this manual are the result of more than twenty years of teaching experience, and courses, workshops, seminars, readings, and personal experiences. The resources that accompany the exercises, activities, and dramatizations in the manual, such as the checklists and activity sheets, help to address the issues of anger and aggressive behaviors, and offer techniques on how to manage them. By using these checklists and activity sheets as frequently as needed, the facilitator will add variety to the program presentations.

People with problems of anger may like the power and control it provides. They may not want to change, but in spite of this, they may be negatively affected by the consequences of their anger. The facilitator should help sell the need to change to reluctant participants. Suggestions and comments from peers may be valuable aspects of this "selling" job.

Program participants should have a minimal reading-skill level. The manual is written on a sixth-grade reading level. However, those with reading skills less than this may profit from the work if directions and examples are read aloud by the facilitator or others in the group. Even those who are nonreaders may benefit from listening to the discussion and role plays.

> Keep in mind that not every individual coming into the program wants to be there. Court orders, parole or probation direction, or even spouses and family may play a role in "convincing" participants to be present. It is important to be patient with these individuals and not come between them and their sources of coercion. Simply stating that, regardless of their reason for attending, you would invite them to make the most out of the meetings and that if they thought about it, they could find some things useful coming out of the sessions.
>
> At the present time, some clinicians are exploring the thorny issues involved with increasing treatment and amenability, but at the present, it is advisable to make do however you can. Some participants will want to genuinely make some changes in their lives, and they will be motivated.

Table of Contents

Foreword by James A. Gondles, Jr. iii
Introduction iv
Definitions of Terms Used in this Guide 1
Issues of Confidentiality 3
Program Rationale 5
Objectives for the Participants/Goals of the Program 6
Individual Approach to the Program 7
Group Approach to the Program 8
Equipment Checklist 12
Facilitator's Role 13
Participant's Role 15
Time Considerations 16
Session Expectations 17
Acronyms 19
Course Overview 20
Flipchart Use 22

Session One on "An Introduction to the Program" 23
    Anger Checklist #1. 29
    Anger Checklist #2. 30

Sessions Two and Three on "Anger Past and Present" 31
    Ideas to Regenerate a Session That Becomes Dull or Boring 35

Role Play Analysis.................................... 40
Role Play Development Sheet 43
Role Play Activity Sheet 44
Postrole Play Group Questions and Discussion Sheet.... 46
Role Play Information Sheet........................... 49
Role Play Activity on The Parking Lot................. 50
Role Play Activity on The Grocery Line 51
Role Play Checklist and Probing Questions 53
Role Reversal Outline 55

Sessions Four and Five on "Anger and Aggression" 56
Role Play Activity on The Flat Tire 60
Role Play Checklist on Anger Detection................ 62
Role Play Checklist on Defusing Cues 63
Role Play Activity on Hockey Revenge 64
Working Backwards Technique 65
Working Backwards Diagram Sheet....................... 68
Working Backwards Question Sheet...................... 69

Sessions Six and Seven on "What Causes Anger?" 70
Role Play Activity on Being Late...................... 74
Role Play Activity on Late to See Parole Officer 75
Case Study Development Sheet 76
Echo Dialog Exercise.................................. 77
Echo Dialog Question Sheet............................ 79

Sessions Eight—Eleven on "How to Manage Your Anger" 80
Role Play Activity on At the Party.................... 87
Role Play Activity on Out of Bounds................... 87
Role Play Activity on Being Cut Off 88

Role Play Activity on Falling. 89
Role Play Activity on A Spilled Drink 89
Role Play Activity on The Restaurant. 90

Session Twelve on "Afterword and Wrap-up" 91
Major Issues. 93
Anger Diet Exercise. 95
Feedback Sheet 96
Feedback to ACA 97
Suggested Readings. 97
Evaluation Form on Each Participant. 99
About the Authors 102

Definitions of Terms Used in this Guide

Anger diet exercise——The exercise name is an upbeat creative use of jargon. The objective is to educate the participants about the dual nature of anger management. The individual should attempt to lose anger calories (aggressive, negative behavior) and increase control vitamins (calming, positive behavior).

Confidentiality——Issue concerning privacy of information.

Echo dialog——This is a self-reflective technique that allows a participant to better focus on and understand what he or she is saying. This technique allows negative self-talk to be verbalized or spoken out loud.

Inside reasons for anger——These have to do with how a person feels or thinks and are subdivided into thinking reasons and feeling reasons.

Negative self-talk——This is talking to yourself in a negative, self-defeating way, which allows your angry thoughts to multiply and possibly become more intense.

Outside reasons for anger——These are things outside or around a person that can make that individual feel angry.

Role play——This is a brief dramatic sketch, which can be used to dramatize angry feelings and behaviors.

Role reversal——After a role play, the facilitator has the option of asking the role player who is acting angry to reverse his or her role. That particular individual may go back into the role play, but now, he or she uses a calming and less aggressive option to deal with the situation.

Signposting anger——This thought-stopping procedure alerts individuals to the body cues and other indications that they are becoming angry.

Working backwards technique——This is a method to be used after a role play or real life incident to help the participant or group reconstruct the situations that led to the angry or aggressive behavior and find ways to avoid such a problem in the future.

Issues of Confidentiality

Part of the adult *Cage Your Rage* program deals with personal questions, anger logs, or diaries. It is important that the facilitator reinforce the view that these items will remain confidential. It is, however, the facilitator's responsibility to check and see that the various activities are done either during group time or as "homework" assignments. The facilitator should advise the participants at the beginning of the program that he or she will need to glimpse quickly at these questions or log entries to assure that they have been completed. There is no specific need for the facilitator to read the entries per se—this is, after all, the participant's writing or communicating to himself or herself.

It is also advisable that the facilitator emphasizes to the group that any situations or events that the group discusses should not be detailed specifically in a personal manner. The facilitator should be aware of potentially awkward and legal ramifications. In some states and provinces, facilitators are mandated to report certain information that they learn. For example, a participant may discuss how he stabbed someone in a drug deal when he became angry, or another participant may state that he was so angry at a neighbor that he broke into the neighbor's house and stole $500 to get even, but he was never caught.

Acting as a facilitator for the program means that you are helping to guide participants to understand anger and how to manage it better. Encourage the group members to speak about everyday aggressive behaviors within legal parameters.

Further explanation on the topic of confidentiality can be obtained by asking your supervisor, director, judge, legal counsel, and parole or probation colleagues. Contact your state, provincial or federal department of corrections or guidance and counseling associations.

The facilitator can suggest that the participant keep details vague and fuzzy in certain questionable instances. Explain to the group what the word "hypothetical" means. Have the group focus on hypothetical situations.

The individual participant should take measures to safeguard the confidential nature of his or her workbook. Some suggestions are as follows:

a) Each group member could keep the workbook with him or her, and then only bring it, as needed or required by the program. The facilitator may require seeing the workbook only every two or three sessions; hence, the participants would not have to have it with them all the time.

b) All participants may wish to use a number or coded symbol to identify the workbook. This number symbol should be known only to them and kept in some obscure part of the book. If the book is lost or stolen, then the individuals will not be readily identified. The facilitator does not know these numbers and, if needed, the facilitator could keep the workbooks under lock.

Program Rationale

Many people who break the law are impatient, frustrated and exhibit aggressive behaviors. If their anger often leaves them with a "short fuse," then their anger is becoming a problem. The adult version of *Cage Your Rage,* like its similar manual *Cage Your Rage for Teens,* is an anger-management program designed to aid participants not only to recognize anger and their aggressive behaviors, but also to give them techniques and ideas to deal with lengthening their "fuse."

It is normal for everyone to become angry from time to time. "Angry" individuals have to realize that no one makes them feel angry—it is their decision. Deciding to become angry or to remain calm can help an individual to make positive changes in his or her life. Ideally, participants in the program must want to change. If this ideal is not achieved initially, then the facilitator can serve as a guide or "direction pointer" actively modeling restraint, confidence, and control.

Objectives for the Participants/Goals of the Program

Doing the activities can accomplish the following:

1. Give the participant the feeling that "I" am doing something about my anger (an improved feeling of confidence and sense of accomplishment).

2. Help the participant be self-educated about how anger works and what can be done about it.

3. Make the participant more responsible for himself or herself.

4. Help the participant control or defuse anger by teaching him or her appropriate techniques to do so (such as "self-talk").

> Due to time considerations, the individual and group method are generally used together to reinforce the participant's progress. An individual program may be used very effectively in a one-to-one situation.

Individual Approach to the Program

There are individual components to the program. The text itself serves as a workbook or diary for the participant. Question sheets, lists, and anger and relaxation logs are included for the individual's use. Paralleling these items are exercises such as checklists and questionnaires that can be given to each participant. Note: A complete individual approach—going through this completely alone—can be an optional or alternate method if an individual refuses to work in a group environment.

> 1. Some individuals do not work well by themselves and need to be monitored closely.
>
> 2. Exercises should be briefly examined to make sure the participants have completed them. This is very important so that program participants offer real answers—not invented ones.
>
> 3. Stress the importance of various activities to the participants.

Group Approach to the Program

The group approach is another way to use the program. In most situations, the group approach is preferred because it is more cost effective and uses peer influence. Group structure, support and interactions can be powerful tools to aid a participant's progress. Often one-to-one attention is not always available due to time and monetary constraints. This program can address anger awareness or anger management on an individual or group basis. An inherent strength of the program's design is that it allows the participant to look at anger from both an individual and group viewpoint.

Group structure can do the following things:

1. Aid participants in working together to help solve anger-related problems

2. Help participants avoid pressure to always come up with an answer

3. Allow activities and exercises, such as role plays, to be performed and analyzed by the group

There are various stages of group development. For example, most models of group development note a resistance stage three or four sessions into the program. If facilitators are aware of this, they can prepare for it and not be caught off guard.

Notes for the Group Leader

1. What you are doing is important. Model this idea by coming to each session prepared and confident.

2. Some participants may not see the importance of a role play or the program itself. You can sell them on its importance.

3. You are in charge of the group. Your aim is to enhance learning that supports anger management—so do not lose your "cool." Most likely, you will be tested!

4. Some participants like to "play games" and behave in a difficult manner. Be aware of this.

5. Some individuals may wish to act out or clown around.

6. A participant may become isolated—even in group activities.

7. Attempt to have small groups—if and whenever possible.

8. You have nothing to fear from the group process. Understand that groups are like sports teams and just need good coaching.

Notes Concerning Groups:

1. Group size is an important consideration. An ideal size might be four-to-six participants. A group of up to eight members could be considered a small group where the opportunity for interaction among the members as well as with the facilitator is enhanced.

    Larger groups consisting of more than eight participants may be divided into smaller groups or teams (teams of two, three, or four). These teams may change in size and members from session to session. These smaller teams may be chosen by the facilitator, initially, and perhaps, later, by the members themselves. It will be the duty of the facilitator to observe and scrutinize team selections closely and if need be, adjust a selection(s) as soon as possible. Individual contribution within the group should be monitored by the facilitator. If it is apparent that one or two members are too dominant, then the facilitator should discuss this with the group(s) involved and make changes to the group(s), if necessary.

2. There is no such thing as an ideal group. Male and female participants mixed together, by itself, do not present a problem. Problems may arise with any size group, but try to keep the group size small.

Group Rules

Group rules may be set by the facilitator or preferably the facilitator and the group together. The facilitator should aim for rules such as the following:

1. Respect other group members' points of view.

2. Avoid rude language or behavior.

3. Agree to make an honest effort with the program.

4. Indicate a time-out if one becomes too upset in a discussion or activity. A facilitator also may wish to indicate this time-out. The facilitator can work together with the group to identify time-out strategies.

5. Each individual must contribute to the group.

6. Eating or drinking coffee/beverages should be reserved for the breaks.

7. Smoking—be aware of the rules at the building concerning smoking.

8. Hats and caps should not be worn during sessions.

> If one or more individuals refuse to follow directions or continually act out, then deal with the problem immediately! Have a one-to-one conversation with the individual(s) and explain that his or her behavior in the group is unacceptable. Tell the participants that you want them to get the most out of the program, but you cannot allow them to jeopardize the progress of the other group members. More than one "warning" may be necessary. Be firm but fair with the individual(s). If he or she persists, bring the issue to the attention of the administration, judge, parole or probation officer.

Equipment Checklist

An equipment checklist is provided for each chapter of the manual. Either the facilitator should bring equipment or make sure that equipment is available at the group-meeting site. This equipment includes:

1. Overhead projector (optional)
2. Transparencies (optional)
3. Camcorder and tape (optional)
4. Video cassette recorder (optional)
5. Flipchart pad and stand
6. Markers
7. Tape recorder and tape (optional)
8. Extra pens/pencils for group members
9. Handouts
10. Extension cord, if needed (optional)
11. Extra bulb for projector (just in case) (optional)
12. *Cage Your Rage* workbook, one copy for each participant

Facilitator's Role

The facilitator helps the program participants to understand the nature of anger and how to be able to manage their anger better. The facilitator should be friendly and approachable, while maintaining a professional attitude. The facilitator should avoid personal examples or angry outbursts. Instead, the facilitator should use general or commonplace reflections. The facilitator should help the participants to accept the program activities and exercises as valuable learning tools—tools that can aid them to curb and control their anger.

> 1. You are only human, and some sessions will run more smoothly than others. Learn from your mistakes, and use your learning to improve future sessions. Remember, what you are doing is important!
>
> 2. For the success of the program, encourage participants to "get into character" during role plays and dramatizations. The idea of the situations and episodes presented is to reflect angry or aggressive behaviors. Emphasize vocal tones and facial expressions to help supplement the presentations. Suggest participants remember past incidents of angry outbursts. This will help the participants to augment any role play or dramatization.

3. Role playing and acting require practice. Therefore, allow time for the participant to develop some proficiency in this area. Be firm but patient in your expectations of participant cooperation and desire to be actively involved in this anger-management program.

4. The facilitator should be conscious of the behavioral norms that realistically might influence the behaviors or attitudes of individual participants or the group as a whole. Specifically, the facilitator must take the time during program preparation to be aware of the developmental influences on participants and consider the possible influences of geographic, cultural, racial, religious, or past experience factors that bias or influence role plays. The possible varieties of issues that these factors could produce are numerous and potentially significant.

It is essential that the facilitator consider this issue and be sensitive to these influences on participants and modify role plays to reduce these influences, where or when appropriate. The facilitator also should be mindful that he or she, as well, is subject to the influence of these characteristics—and they may be different from those of the participants.

Participant's Role

The participant should be open to change and make an honest effort to contribute to group activities. A participant should understand that the program is designed to help him or her make better decisions when confronted with becoming angry or volatile. A key role for each participant is to understand and accept responsibility for his or her actions.

Learning about anger and its causes and respecting the "other" person's point of view reinforce the idea of becoming responsible for one's own anger management. Learning techniques and ideas to help curb angry feelings and aggressive behaviors help to make the participant capable of becoming a responsible "anger manager."

Time Considerations

Each group a facilitator deals with will be unique. Therefore, it is difficult to accurately anticipate the length of time needed to adequately complete activities, questions, and discussions from one group or session to the next. After the facilitator uses the manual, he or she will become more familiar with the time elements of the program and adapt and adjust them as required. A few minutes at the end of each session should be used for a review of the main points of that session.

There are six sections in the text of *Cage Your Rage* that coincide with the accompanying anger-management program. The text is divided into twelve sessions.

Introduction	...one session
Chapter 1	...two sessions
Chapter 2	...two sessions
Chapter 3	...two sessions
Chapter 4	...four sessions
Afterword	...one session

The sessions should be from sixty to seventy-five minutes in length. The facilitator can choose to do two sessions per week for six weeks or one session a week for twelve weeks. Other strategies also may be devised by the facilitator, as needed.

Session Expectations

The chapters of *Cage Your Rage* are divided into twelve sessions. One session is allocated for the introduction to the program—the foreword to the book. Two sessions are needed for Chapters 1, 2, and 3. Four sessions are allotted for the fourth chapter, and one session is set for the afterword or wrap-up.

It is imperative that the facilitator consider and anticipate the participants' potential shyness, hesitancy, and self-consciousness about being involved in such activities as role playing. Initial resistance by part or all of the group to some exercises is usual. The facilitator, as the leader, should attempt to allay the participants' fears. It is helpful if the leader exhibits patience, sensitivity, and understanding concerning these fears—particularly during the beginning sessions of the program. The participants should be reminded continually that the program is designed to educate and help them better understand their angry thoughts and aggressive behaviors. The facilitator should expect to model some role plays himself or herself. The facilitator should allow time for the participants to practice warm-up exercises for the various role plays.

Telling a few jokes or anecdotes at the beginning of a session can aid a facilitator in giving the participants the opportunity to relax and, in general, help to create a positive atmosphere. The facilitator should be sensitive to the cultural, ethnic, and racial background of the group members when, and if any joke-telling occurs.

Exercises involving making-up role plays, filling out case-study development sheets, and answering questions may pose some problems for both the facilitator and the participants. Many of the problems may be alleviated if done in a group atmosphere that allows for individual input.

Group work should be guided and directed by the facilitator and include all group members, while at the same time staying in tune with the activity's theme. The facilitator should remain positive and reassuring while encouraging individual response within the group setting.

Leading the program means that one can expect some sessions to be more successful than others. It is essential that the facilitator avoid becoming too frustrated and, instead, concentrate on the central purpose of the program. The program aims to help the participants to recognize angry thoughts and aggressive behaviors while, at the same time, teaching them techniques to become better anger managers. The fact that this effort is being made is, in itself, important—the facilitator's contribution in making this effort is commendable and, in fact, is essential in helping the participants to help themselves.

Acronyms

The following acronyms may help those using the program by helping participants focus on a concept through the use of an acronym. These acronyms may be interwoven throughout the sessions.

CAN: Control Anger Now

TEAM: Together Eliminate Angry Moments

ANGER: Anger Non-aggression Group Effective Response

ARC: Anger Response Controls

I AM: Individual Anger Management

GOAL: Get Our Anger Licked

Course Overview

This program has six sections, consisting of twelve sessions (usually sixty to seventy minutes in length).

1. **Introduction to the Program (1 session)**
   Here the facilitator and participants meet. The facilitator tells the participants that they have an important role to play in dealing with their anger. Secondly, the facilitator tells them that going through the various activities and exercises will be something they can do both within the group as well as in their residences or with friends.

2. **Chapter 1—Anger: Past and Present (2 sessions)**
   The focus in these sessions is on what anger is and how it may have developed in an individual's past, as well as how it continues through to the present. The facilitator should emphasize that everyone experiences anger differently, but what is important to show is how an individual chooses to deal with anger, and how excessive anger separates a normal feeling of anger from an explosive one.

3. **Chapter 2—Anger and Aggression (2 sessions)**
   These sessions deal with the relation between anger and aggression. The facilitator helps participants understand the ideal that anger has good and bad points. In the session, ways to stop angry feelings from becoming a problem are explored as well.

4. Chapter 3—What Causes Anger? (2 session)
   This section centers around the causes of anger, which are divided into two main categories: "Outside Reasons" and "Inside Reasons." The facilitator helps participants learn how these various reasons can contribute to an individual's feelings of anger.

5. Chapter 4—How to Manage Your Anger (4 sessions)
   Managing one's anger is the central theme of this chapter. The facilitator helps participants learn techniques to help them deal with angry feelings and aggressive behaviors. The facilitator emphasizes the idea that by actively working on problem-solving abilities coupled with keeping one's frustration level low, anger can be managed.

6. Afterword and Wrap-up (1 session)
   The aim of this session is to review the ideas learned in the program and evaluate the participant's growth in knowing and using these skills.

Flipchart Use

- Be neat.
- Preferably print rather than write.
- Prepare ideas in advance—have them written down and then put them on the flipchart during the session.
- Be brief (use point form whenever possible).
- Print large enough so that all participants may easily see ideas.
- Avoid standing directly in front of the flipchart while either writing on it or pointing out items.
- Have extra markers on hand. Use a variety of colors, especially black, red and blue.
- You may wish to have two flipcharts: One for making points and ideas; the other for writing down comments or questions from the participants or for yourself to look at later.

Session One on "An Introduction to the Program"

Target Group: Adult males and females

Time Allocation: One session (60 to 75 minutes)

Requirements: Chairs (tables optional) should be set in a small but workable "U" or semicircle shape. An additional small space should be used to conduct role play activities.

Performance Indicators: Each participant should know the following at the end of this module:
1. Why they are in this program
2. How anger has impeded them in the past
3. That there are alternatives to explosions of anger

Assessment Procedures:
1. Feedback from exercises and activities
2. Question and answer format

Methods:
1. Group discussion
2. Lecture
3. Goal setting
4. Paper and pencil exercise

Training supplies, aids, and equipment:

1. Flipchart pad and stand
2. Markers
3. Extra pens and pencils for group members
4. Handouts:
   - Index cards or sheets of paper for goals
   - Anger Checklists (pages 29-30)
   - Blank paper for describing angry incident
5. Sufficient copies of *Cage Your Rage* workbook so each participant has one

Summary of Introduction

The theme in this introduction is to convince the participants that they have a stake in changing their customary methods of dealing with anger. The secondary purpose is to show participants that going through the exercises in this book will be something that they can do. Many of them even may enjoy the activities. The objective is that by the end of this first session participants should be familiar with the contents of the introduction in *Cage Your Rage*, pages 1-3, and be able to tell how anger has impeded them. They should also be able to tell why running away from problems or fearful emotions does not always work. Ideally, participants will be curious about the program and excited about participating in it.

Introduction to the program (Session 1)

1. Introduce yourself (2 minutes).

2. Explain confidentiality (5 minutes).

3. Ask each participant to introduce himself or herself and to provide some background details (15 minutes).

4. Outline the program's goals and objectives. Use a short lecture and flipchart (10 minutes).

5. Warm-up activity: Ask each participant to give an example of a time that he or she was angry in the last month. Ask what triggered the anger and how the individual dealt with this situation. (7 to 10 minutes).

6. Lead a general discussion of anger (Note: the previous warm-up activity should help the discussion) (10 minutes).

7. Provide a break (10 minutes).

8. Discuss various program exercises, checklists, and activities (especially role plays). Hand out *Cage Your Rage* workbooks. Note the areas for diary entries in the workbooks (10 minutes).

9. Instruct participants to set up personal program goals (10 minutes). Use index cards or sheets of paper. Then, collect each participant's goal sheet. Review them. At the next session, comment on goals. Some goal sheets may be returned to participants to redo.

10. Pass out Anger Checklist #1 (page 29). Ask participants to complete it (2-5 minutes). The facilitator collects and keeps this sheet until the last session in the program, when it is given back to the participant and reviewed.

Optional Activities

1. Discussing anger. The facilitator should narrate a generalized scenario about a time he or she was angry.

2. Drawing illustration of an angry situation, especially on the anger checklist.

Working the Program

1. Participant Introduction

    The facilitator should ask all participants to give their names and some background information (such as age, activities or hobbies they may have). Encourage the participants to share pertinent additional information. Do not, however, push the individuals too hard to divulge personal information if they choose not to voluntarily disclose.

    Each person, beginning with the facilitator, is asked to indicate one positive point about himself or herself. The atmosphere should be relaxed but informative.

2. The facilitator should explain issues of confidentiality—and ask group members to relate hypothetical instances (pages 3-4 of this manual). The facilitator should ask group members to keep confidential the issues discussed in the group.

3. Each member of the group, beginning with the facilitator, should share instances of a time when he or she was angry.

4. It is important that the situation described by the facilitator be something to which the participants can relate.

5. The facilitator should explain that anger is a normal emotion. However, sometimes our anger may cause us to act out—to do something that is hurtful. Some people may lash out physically—hitting, kicking, or using weapons. Others may yell, swear, or say nasty or hurtful things. Sometimes, either of these responses to anger gets a reaction from another person. This

reaction may get you in trouble: first, with yourself and second, with the other person or persons, and possibly with the authorities—including the police.

6. The facilitator should distribute one copy of *Cage Your Rage* workbook to each group member. The facilitator should allow time for individuals to examine the book and make comments about it. Individuals should put their name or identifying number on the book (pages 3-4 on "Confidentiality").

7. The facilitator should explain the purpose of the program—to put the individual back in charge of his or her own life and not get sidetracked by emotions of anger (page 6, "Objectives for the Participants.")

8. The facilitator should outline how the group will proceed through the twelve sessions or other arrangement of the aspects of this book and the expected results both for the group and the individuals involved.

   Some of the group expectations include:
   - The group will complete the activities and exercises in the book.
   - The group will learn about anger and alternative responses to both anger and aggression.

   For the individual, the idea is that the individual will be more in charge of himself or herself and have more ways to respond to situations that in the past had stirred up his or her anger. Additionally, the individual will learn new ways to relax—without alcohol or other drugs.

9. The facilitator should ask individuals to write about an incident of anger on a separate page. This anger incident will be referred

to again in the final session. Group members may choose to graphically illustrate their anger situation. The facilitator should collect these descriptions and hand them back at the final session.

10. The facilitator will distribute the Anger Checklists (pages 29-30) as a pretest. At the end of the program, in the final session, each individual will retake it and see if there have been changes.

The facilitator should tell individuals that they may wish to illustrate the back of the Anger Checklists with their own art. The facilitator will collect the completed forms and store them in a secure area until the final session of the program when they will be returned to the program participants so that they will be able to see the progress that they have made.

The facilitator may wish to assign the reading of Chapter 1 as an assignment to be done before the next session.

> The facilitator should emphasize the need for honesty in answers—the objective is to help participants find alternative methods for handling their own anger so that they can be more successful. The idea is not to discover who is the most angry or the nastiest person.
>
> Throughout the sessions, the facilitator should emphasize how this program will empower the individual—increase the choices available to him or her in most situations and show why this is a positive goal. The objective is to build enthusiasm for the rest of the sessions of the program so that individuals look forward to them.

Anger Checklist #1

Note: The following Anger Checklists may be reproduced for handouts.

_____
(fill in name and date)

1. I become frustrated easily. ____ Yes ____ No

2. Things often irritate me. ____ Yes ____ No

3. Being called a name really upsets me. ____ Yes ____ No

4. I shout a lot when I am angry. ____ Yes ____ No

5. I often get so angry I want to lash out. ____ Yes ____ No

6. I often talk myself into situations I later regret. ____ Yes ____ No

7. I bottle up my feelings when I am upset. ____ Yes ____ No

8. I do not stop to consider the consequences when I am involved in an argument. ____ Yes ____ No

9. I feel I get upset easily. ____ Yes ____ No

10. I have been angry at someone today. ____ Yes ____ No

Anger Checklist #2

_____
(fill in name and date)

1. I have a good sense of humor. ____ Yes ____ No

2. I take deep breaths when I feel extremely angry. ____ Yes ____ No

3. I use self-talk (talk to myself) to help me from losing my temper. ____ Yes ____ No

4. During a discussion or argument, I talk calmly—even though I am upset. ____ Yes ____ No

5. I stay calm if someone calls me a name. ____ Yes ____ No

6. I listen openly to another person's view even if I am arguing with that person. ____ Yes ____ No

7. I can meet someone halfway in an argument. ____ Yes ____ No

8. I have told someone a joke today. ____ Yes ____ No

9. I am in control of my anger. ____ Yes ____ No

10. I can laugh at a joke or insult that is directed at me. ____ Yes ____ No

Sessions Two and Three on "Anger Past and Present"

Target Group: Adult males and females

Time Allocation: Two sessions (60 to 75 minutes each)

Requirements: Chairs (tables optional) should be set in a small but workable "U" or semicircle shape. An additional small space should be used to conduct role play activities.

Performance Indicators: Each participant should know the following at the end of this module:
1. What anger is
2. How anger developed in this individual's past and continues to the present
3. That an individual has a choice in how he or she chooses to deal with anger

Methods:
1. Lecture
2. Role plays
3. Question and answer sheets
4. Group discussion
5. Exercises to aid participant's understanding of the subject matter

Training supplies, aids, and equipment:

1. Overhead projector (optional)
2. Transparencies (optional)
3. Camcorder and tape (optional)
4. Video cassette recorder (optional)
5. Flipchart stand and pad
6. Markers
7. Tape recorder and tape (optional)
8. Extra pens and pencils for group members
9. Handouts:
    - Role Play Development Sheet (page 43)
    - Postrole Play Group Question and Discussion Sheet (pages 46-48)
    - Role Play Checklist and Probing Questions (pages 53-55)
10. Lined paper for writing
11. Sufficient copies of *Cage Your Rage* workbook to distribute to each participant
12. Extension cord (if needed) (optional)
13. Extra bulb for projector (just in case) (optional)

Summary of Chapter 1: "Anger Past and Present"

The theme of this chapter is to get participants to discuss what anger is and how it may have developed in one's past and how it continues through to the present. Anger is depicted as a "human emotion—similar to joy or sadness." Everyone experiences forms of anger from time to time. It is, however, the way one chooses to deal with anger that separates someone with a normal anger response from a person with more explosive aggressive behavior.

Keeping angry feelings bottled up or having a short "fuse" could magnify the tendency of some individuals to react in a spontaneous, negative manner. Such individuals may be unable to channel their angry impulses properly; they lash out verbally or physically against themselves or others. Sometimes an individual grows up with anger within the family. Aggressive actions or verbalizations may be made by others with whom one interacts, including parents or siblings.

Chapter 1 (Session 2)

1. Facilitator reviews the key points from the prior lesson, introduces today's session objectives and key points (3-5 minutes).

2. Selected participants read Chapter 1 of *Cage Your Rage* aloud (15 minutes).

3. Facilitator demonstrates role plays and holds a follow-up discussion (5 minutes).

4. Facilitator conducts warm-up activity (page 39). The participants become involved with this activity after the facilitator models a short role play (7-10 minutes).

5. Participants discuss Role Play Analysis (page 40) (10 minutes).

6. Participants perform Role Play Activity on "The Parking Lot" (page 50) (15 minutes).

7. Provide a break (10 minutes).

8. Participants complete the Role Play Checklist and Probing Questions (pages 53-55) (15 minutes).

Chapter 1 (Session 3)

1. Facilitator reviews the last session (lecture method using flipcharts) (2 minutes).

2. Facilitator introduces today's session objectives and key points (lecture method using flipcharts) (3-5 minutes).

3. Facilitator conducts a warm-up activity. Ask the participants to relate a time when they were involved in an angry situation that worked out well. How did this happen? Ask each participant to focus the explanation on the person, not the problem. This exercise can be repeated (7-10 minutes).

4. Participants perform Role Play Activity on "The Grocery Line" (pages 51-52) or use the Role Play Development Sheet (page 43) to invent a realistic role play (15 minutes).

5. Participants complete the Role Play Checklist and Probing Questions (pages 53-55) (15 minutes).

6. Provide a break (10 minutes).

7. Participants complete the role-reversal activity on "The Grocery Line" (pages 51-52). It is important that the facilitator model the first role-reversal technique by doing a short role play himself or herself and then reversing the role (2 minutes).

8. Participants make workbook entries in *Cage Your Rage* (pages 4-22). Instruct them to finish up on their own before the next session (10 minutes).

> The facilitator should remind participants:
> Do not keep angry feelings bottled up inside. This can create a "backfire" effect that can serve to ignite a "short fuse" with potentially aggressive or explosive results.
> Do not become a puppet, because that allows others to pull your strings. You can learn ways to help defuse your "anger detonator." The step along this path is to become responsible for yourself. Take control and do not let someone else "string" you along!

Initially, the facilitator's job may be difficult, but it does not have to be impossible. You are providing a service to the participants, institutions, and society in general. Small setbacks can be anticipated but also can be used as springboards of experience for future sessions and programs. It is important to constantly accentuate the positives, no matter how small.

If a session finishes too soon or drags on, the facilitator may wish to have the participants more involved by developing a role play (Role Play Development Sheet, page 43). The facilitator may allow two participants to work together.

Ideas to Regenerate a Session That Becomes Dull or Boring

Note: Although these are optional ideas, they can instill interest and enthusiasm in the group process.

- A facilitator can interject a lively, imaginative anecdote. He or she can become a story-teller relating some anger-laden episode (real or imagined). Basically, "spin a tall tale" to create interest.

The themes to these stories may be prepared in advance and used at the appropriate time.

Use some "what if" scenarios, such as the following:

1. What if your car is stolen?

2. What if you lose a phone number and do not know how to find the original number again?

3. What if your probation officer does not believe you, even though you are not lying?

4. What if you are taken to the judge or parole office for an infraction and have all of your privileges revoked?

5. What if your best friend steals your date or cheats with your spouse?

- Be prepared to either video or audio-tape a role play during a session. Also, be prepared to play it back during any future session (particularly, when the participants seem bored or lack interest).

- Digress and discuss an upcoming big event or activity (such as a sporting event, concert, or movie). Try to captivate the group's interest and allow a short discussion of the event. After a few minutes remark, "That's interesting" or "That sounds great." Now, re-route to program activities and goals by saying, "Would you be disappointed if the concert were cancelled at the last minute?" "How would you feel if the ball game were rained out in the seventh inning and the score was tied at 6-6?"

- If the participants become disinterested, the facilitator may wish to employ a past activity or exercise in the program that had been successful. The facilitator may wish to keep a four-point success chart on all activities and exercises done throughout the program. "One" indicates little or no success; "two" indicates fair; "three" represents good; and "four" is an excellent rating.

- Allow a participant to be a news reporter interviewing you, the facilitator, just after you have:

    a. smashed the brand new car that you had just bought
    b. just missed the plane because the taxi driver had a flat
    c. just locked yourself out of your apartment or house—forgetting all of your money and keys

- Use the Role Play Development Sheet (page 43) to develop more role plays with group input.

General Questions and Considerations

1. Anticipate potential questions that may be asked in a given session.

2. Vary the types of questions you ask.

3. Include all of the participants in the question/answer period.

4. Questions may have to be more simplified at times, requiring simply a "yes" or "no" answer, whenever the group is generally unresponsive.

5. Use more in-depth or diagnostic questions when participants are speaking freely and are eager to give input.

6. If a participant continually asks the facilitator "What do you think?," reply by noting that what you think is not as important in this situation as the participant's observations on the topic. Follow up with "Your thoughts on this are important, and I feel that they should be heard."

7. A participant may purposefully try to ask "off the topic" or "off the wall" types of questions. Simply note that they may have a point there and ask them to answer the question that you asked (that was on the topic) a moment ago. Another comment may be "Yes, you may have a point; perhaps we could consider it more closely at the end of the session."

8. Derailing questions may surface, such as "Why do we have to do this anyway?" The facilitator should realize that these types of questions may be being asked to test the facilitator, or possibly because the individual actually feels that the program is of little or no value. In any case, the response should be firm and genuine. "The material covered in this program is valuable and can serve to help everybody who wishes to better manage his or her anger." The facilitator can use this opportunity to restate the program goals and objectives to the entire group.

> Remember, no participant has the right to continually jeopardize the potential success of the other individuals in the group. If a participant persists, and seems intent on sabotaging the program, then it will be necessary to approach the director or superintendent, the parole officer, or other programming staff (as the case might be) and express your concerns.

Reading the Text

The facilitator may have assigned the reading of this chapter to be done before participants get to the session. Realistically, many of them will not have done it. Therefore, it may be helpful to have group participants read the book aloud and allow time for them to complete the exercises. Note: Be sure not to embarrass those individuals whose reading skills are low. Ask for volunteers to do the reading. If there are none, the facilitator may read until the group gets bored with the facilitator's voice and someone decides to volunteer.

Writing Responses

Writing personal responses to the text questions is very important. The facilitator should check to be sure this has been done.

Warm-ups for Role Plays and Dramatizations

The following ideas are suggestions to set the mood for playing a role. The warm-ups should take about ten minutes. These warmups can be done in a group setting; the facilitator asks various members for a response to the following situations:

- How would you act if you were sad?

- How would you act if you won a million dollars?

- How would you act if you lost twenty dollars?

- Imagine that you did not have to go to work this Friday, how would you act?

- You just shot the winning basket that helps your team to win the city championship—describe how you would feel.

The Use of Role Play

A typical role play is between three-to-five minutes in length. They may run longer after the participants gain more practice. The facilitator should intervene in the role play whenever he or she feels that it is becoming "bogged down" or ineffective. Encouragement and a word or two of advice by the facilitator may help keep the participants enlivened. Discussion and follow-up exercises and activities are also part of the role-play process. Ideas for follow up are presented with the role play activities for each activity.

A role play is a brief dramatic sketch, which can be used to dramatize angry feelings and behaviors. Program participants may be broken up into groups of twos, threes, or other numbers to help develop a role play. Personal insights and general experience can be offered by group members to help generate role play setups.

Initial role plays should attempt to be short—ranging from one-to-three minutes in length. The Role Play Development Sheet (page 43) will aid the participants in the development of their role play. (That page may be reproduced.) Particular attention should be given to the quality of the responses of the postrole play question section. (The Postrole Play Group Questions and Discussion Sheet on pages 46-48 may be reproduced.)

Keep numbers low in groups designing role plays. Initially, it may be best to start with pairs of participants with the facilitator as one of the pairs.

Optional: the role play does not have to be acted out but may serve as a case study (imaginary) to be discussed by the whole group.

Role Play Analysis (length of time: 15 minutes)

Look at an incident, episode, or situation where a person's anger might arise or be triggered.

Some of the following may help you:

1. An embarrassing moment.
    Example:
    - You open a can of cola and it sprays all over you. The can had been shaken up previously, but you did not realize it. Now, people all around you are laughing, and you feel embarrassed and enraged. Anger is a secondary feeling. What did you feel first—embarrassed? scared?

2. Negative self-talk (talking to yourself in a negative, self-defeating way: this allows your angry thoughts to multiply and possibly become more intense).
    Examples:
    - "Why do things always have to happen to me?"
    - "I'm sick and tired of it!"
    - "If one more thing happens to me, just one more, I'm going to explode."

3. Frustrating, irritable, or annoying episodes.
    Example:
    - John's driving license has been suspended for driving while intoxicated. He has a car, but he cannot drive it for six months. He is late for work, and he has missed his bus. He becomes very frustrated and decides to take his car. "Who cares what the law says," he thinks. "I have to get to work. I'll drive my car anyway!"

4. Verbal abuse situations can serve as the basis for developing a role play. Some examples of this might include the following situations:
    Examples:
    - An individual is being called names or being spoken to in a derogatory manner.

- Family members of an individual are being called names. A negative reference to one's mother may prompt an angry or potentially violent outburst by an individual. Of course, cultural sensitivity must be kept in mind when dealing with groups and minorities. Cultural sensitivity is an important consideration during all discussions on anger management.

5. Sometimes a person's hope can lead an individual to expect too much, too often. When things go wrong, the anxiety and frustration level may trigger an angry response.

    Example:
    - You thought you were doing well. You were working week-ends, playing on the basketball team, and doing well at your local community college. However, now things have changed. Jim broke up with you. You cannot get your mind on school anymore and you've been late for work five times in two months. Your basketball coach says you are missing too many tournaments on the weekends. You told her that you work, but she does not understand. You are tired, depressed, and fed up.

6. Ask participants to list and then describe their own ideas. Hand out copies of the Role Play Development Sheet for them to write their description.

7. Ask group members to briefly describe an incident that triggers their anger. This may be done orally or written on a sheet of paper.

Role Play Development Sheet

    Role Play Characters: Names   Age

1.

2.

3.

4.

Briefly describe each character. Give each character in the role play a name.

1.

2.

3.

4.

Describe the situation:

_____

_____

_____

_____

_____

Role Play Dialog:

1. The dialog may be improvised or made up as the role play unfolds.
2. Dialog also may be organized and written down beforehand.

The dialog may be written down and discussed without the role play being acted out. Use an overhead projector for this option.

Role Play Activity Sheet

1. Describe the conflict.

   _____

   _____

   _____

2. Describe the participants.

   _____

   _____

   _____

   _____

   _____

   _____

3. List group suggestions for positive alternatives to defuse the situation.

_____

_____

_____

_____

_____

4. Use the Role Play Checklist and Probing Questions.

_____

_____

_____

_____

_____

_____

_____

Postrole Play Group Questions and Discussion Sheet

1. Identify angry feelings or aggressive behavior evident in the role play.

    a.

    b.

    c.

    d.

    e.

    f.

2. Identify choices that could have helped to defuse the character's anger in the role play.

    a.

    b.

    c.

    d.

    e.

    f.

3. When would you have suggested a "time-out" to the character to help defuse his or her anger?

_____

_____

_____

_____

4. How would you have played the lead character differently in that situation?

_____

_____

_____

_____

5. Give examples of positive self-talk that the main character might have employed. Note: Positive self-talk means to say things to yourself to help you defuse your angry feelings and aggressive behaviors in a given situation.
    Examples:
    - I must stay calm.
    - Wait a minute.
    - I have nothing to prove.

- This is not worth it.
- I must take some deep breaths.

_____

_____

_____

_____

6. What advice could you give to the main character to help him or her from getting angry in this situation if it were to happen again?

_____

_____

_____

_____

_____

_____

Role Play Information Sheet

Role Player's Duties:

1. Participate by assuming a given role.

2. Focus attention on the role.

3. Try to see yourself in that situation.

4. Use past anger experiences or ideas from the text.

5. Indicate a time-out, if needed.

6. Remember to be yourself—the role play itself is just an acting exercise to enhance learning about anger and discussing it.

The Goal of the Role Play

The objective is to simulate upsetting or "heated" situations involving anger but to do so in a controlled setting. This will enable the group to look at and discuss anger-provoking situations but also focus on ways to use positive defusing techniques and methods.

> ### Role Play Discussion
>
> The facilitator should guide the discussion, allowing each group member to contribute. Group members should identify angry or aggressive behaviors as well as any calming or defusing attempts. Refer to the Role Play Checklist and Probing Questions (page 53-55) to reinforce the discussion.

Role Play Activity on The Parking Lot

Length of time: 15 minutes, including 5 minutes for the role play itself.

1. Event: You are trying to find a parking space at a mall.

2. Number of Participants: two—you, and the driver of another vehicle.

3. Situation: You are tired at the end of a long week. The Christmas season is quickly approaching; people seem to be out at every store and mall buying gifts. You have been driving around the parking lot and can't seem to find a single space to park. Finally, someone up ahead backs out. You gladly wait for them.

    Suddenly, a car comes zooming from the other direction and takes your space before you can pull in. Your blinker was on and you had waited patiently for that spot—no way are you going to let this go. You drive up behind the other car, open your door and say to yourself, "I'll straighten this clown out."

4. Ask for group suggestions for positive alternatives to defuse the situation.

5. Use the Postrole Play Group Questions and Discussion Sheet (pages 46-48).

6. Use the Role Play Checklist and Probing Questions (pages 53-55). **Note:** This form may be reproduced.

Role Play Activity on The Grocery Line

Length of time: 15 minutes, including 2-5 minutes for the role play itself.

1. Event: You are in a long line at a grocery store.

2. Number of participants: three—you, a woman in the line in front of you named Joan, and a friend of Joan's named Sue.

3. Situation: Work was particularly hectic today and all you really want to do is get home and sit down on your reclining chair and relax. However, you need a few things for supper, and guests are coming in for the long weekend. You stop in at the grocery store and hope it won't take too long. To your dismay, when you go to the check-out counter the lines are unbelievably long. Your patience is thin and you have better things to do than stand in a stupid line. But you have no choice and do a slow burn as the line moves ever so slowly.

    You notice a woman in line calling to a friend named Joan. Joan says, "Hello Mary. Aren't these lines dreadful?"

    Mary responds, "Yes they are. Would you like to go in front of me?"

    Joan says, "That would be great. Thank you Mary." Joan now positions her loaded cart next to Mary and starts to move in front of her.

    No way! She's no better than anyone else! You walk down to where Mary and Joan are standing and you growl, "Who do you think you are?"

4. Ask for group suggestions for positive alternatives to defuse the situation.

5. Use the Postrole Play Group Questions and Discussion Sheet (pages 46-48).

6. Use the Role Play Checklist and Probing Questions (pages 53-55). **Note:** This form may be reproduced.

7. Instruct participants to be prepared for the next session by reading Chapter 2 in *Cage Your Rage* workbook.

Role Play Checklist and Probing Questions

A. Checklist Questions

1. Was the "angry" dialog realistic? ____Yes ____No

2. Could you identify with or relate to the anger shown? ____Yes ____No

3. Have you ever been in a similar situation? ____Yes ____No

4. Do you feel you would have been very angry in the given situation? ____Yes ____No

5. Would you have reacted differently? ____Yes ____No

B. Probing Questions

1. The main problem in this situation was

   _____

   _____

   _____

2. List three angry or aggressive behaviors used in the role play.

   a. _____

b. _____

c. _____

3. Which behavior do you think was the key to the situation becoming potentially worse?

_____

_____

_____

4. List three positive or calming influences exhibited by the role players.

a. _____

b. _____

c. _____

5. What positive or calming behavior did you think was most beneficial in helping to defuse the situation?

_____

_____

_____

_____

_____

Role Reversal Outline

After a role play, the facilitator has the option of asking the role player who is acting angry to reverse his or her role. That particular individual may go back into the role play, but now, he or she uses a calming and less aggressive option to deal with the situation.

- Perhaps another member of the group may take the angry-role player spot either immediately or later in the role play.

- Use the Role Play Activity Sheet here again, if needed.

Sessions Four and Five on "Anger and Aggression"

Target Group: Adult males and females

Time Allocation: Two sessions (60 to 75 minutes each)

Requirements: Chairs (tables optional) should be set in a small but workable "U" or semicircle shape. An additional small space should be used to conduct role play activities.

Performance Indicators: Each participant should know the following at the end of this module:
1. Anger has both good and bad points
2. Some ways to stop angry feelings from becoming a problem
3. The relationship between anger and aggression

Assessment Procedures:
1. Feedback from exercises and activities
2. Question and answer format

Methods:
1. Lecture
2. Role Plays
3. Question and answer sheets
4. Group discussion
5. Exercises to aid the participants' understanding of the subject matter

Training supplies, aids, and equipment:

1. Overhead projector (optional)
2. Transparencies (optional)
3. Camcorder and tape (optional)
4. Video cassette recorder (optional)
5. Flipchart pad and stand
6. Markers
7. Tape recorder and tape (optional)
8. Extra pens/pencils for group members
9. Handouts
    - Role Play Development Sheet (page 43)
    - Postrole Play Group Questions and Discussion Sheet (pages 46-48)
    - Role Play Checklist and Probing Questions (pages 53-55)
    - Role Play Activity Sheet (pages 44-45) (optional)
    - Role Reversal Outline (page 55) (optional)
    - Working Backwards Diagram Sheet (page 68) (optional) Working Backwards Question Sheet (page 69) (optional)
    - Role Play Checklist on Anger Detection (page 62)
    - Role Play Checklist on Defusing Cues (page 63)
10. Sufficient copies of *Cage Your Rage* workbook to distribute one copy to each participant
11. Extension cord (if needed) (optional)
12. Extra bulb for projector (just in case) (optional)

Summary of Chapter 2: "Anger and Aggression"

Anger and aggression often become interwoven. The emotion called "anger" can give way to aggressive behavior unless our feelings are funneled or redirected. It then becomes necessary to examine the relationship between anger and aggression.

Anger has both good and bad points. One good point is that anger may supply a person with energy to deal with a dangerous situation. A bad point is that anger may stop a person from thinking, feeling, and acting clearly. It is important that one understands both the good and bad aspects of anger.

Chapter 2 (Session 4)

1. Review the last session (lecture method with flipchart) (2 minutes).
2. Introduce today's session objectives and key points from *Cage Your Rage* (lecture method with flipchart) (5-10 minutes).
3. Warm-up exercise: Think of a situation where someone may have borrowed something from you (such as sneakers or a t-shirt) and returned it in poor condition. What might you do about this? How might you react? Ask each participant (7-10 minutes).
4. Participants perform Role Play Activity on "The Flat Tire" (pages 60-61) (15 minutes).
5. Participants should complete the Checklist on Anger Detection (page 62) (10 minutes). Refer back to "The Flat Tire" role play.
6. Provide a break (10 minutes).
7. Participants complete Postrole Play Group Questions and Discussion sheet (page 46-48) (15 minutes).
8. Participants start making the workbook entries in *Cage Your Rage* (pages 32-36) (10 minutes).

Chapter Two (session 5)

1. Review the last session (lecture method with flipchart) (2 minutes).
2. Introduce today's session objectives and key points from *Cage Your Rage* workbook (lecture method with flipchart) (5-10 minutes).
3. Warm-up Activity: Ask a participant to give an example of a time when he or she became angry with a group of people. What happened? How did the person react? Would he or she have reacted differently if only one other person, rather than a group of people, had been present? Was he or she embarrassed? Did this contribute to the anger? Repeat this exercise with a few other participants (7-10 minutes).
4. Participants perform the Role Play Activity on "Hockey Revenge" (page 64) (15 minutes).
5. Participants should complete the Checklist on Defusing Cues (page 63) (10 minutes).
6. Provide a break (10 minutes).
7. Participants should complete the workbook entries for *Cage Your Rage* (pages 32-36) (10 minutes).

Controlling anger and aggression comes from knowing how they work.

The individual has a choice—to either ignore an irritation or get angry about it. There is also a third option. The individual can choose to deal with an irritation in an appropriate manner. This is one of the goals of this program.

To avoid anger becoming a problem, do not bombard yourself with angry feelings and then allow them to snowball into aggressive actions. Where angry feelings are concerned, "Look before you leap." Attempt to avoid the frequency and intensity of angry feelings from consuming you.

Optional Activity Consideration

1. Use the Role Play Activity Sheet (pages 44-45) to make up or set up a role-play episode. Such sheets should be made available during the sessions dealing with this chapter.

2. Use the Role Reversal Outline (page 55) with any role play. Sheets should be made available in sessions dealing with this chapter.

3. Use the Postrole Play Group Questions and Discussion Sheet (pages 46-48) with any role play. It may be helpful to have these sheets available or a transparency copy of this form ready for use on the overhead projector.

4. Introduce the Working Backwards Technique (page 65). Do the exercise with an anger situation suggested by participants.

Role Play Activity on The Flat Tire

Length of time: 15 minutes, including 2 to 5 minutes for the role play itself.

1. Event: You are returning from a trip.

2. Number of Participants: one—yourself.

3. Situation: You have been away for the weekend on a trip. You have promised your girlfriend that you would be back early Sunday night. You are going to celebrate your one-year anniversary of going together. You intend to take her to dinner and a movie. Your girlfriend was happy that you remembered the anniversary and is looking forward to the dinner.

You are running late as you drive off to pick her up. "Oh no!" A small explosion indicates that you have a flat tire. You carefully guide the car to the side of the road. You are upset—now you'll be late for sure. You walk around and open the trunk to discover you forgot to put the spare back in after taking it out to make room for your luggage. You are enraged and start kicking the car.

4. Ask for group suggestions for positive alternatives to defuse the situation.

5. Orally go through the Postrole Play Group Questions and Discussion Sheet (pages 46-48).

6. Introduce and go through the Role Play Checklist on Anger Detection (next page).

7. Introduce and go through the Role Play Checklist on Defusing Cues (page 63).

8. Instruct participants to read Chapter 3 "What Causes Anger?" in *Cage Your Rage* workbook for the next session. If there is time during the session, they may begin doing this.

Role Play Checklist on Anger Detection

The goal is to detect angry or aggressive behavior by using this checklist.

1. Was the role player talking loudly? ____Yes ____No

2. Was the participant unwilling to compromise? ____Yes ____No

3. Did the participant refuse to accept responsibility for the situation? ____Yes ____No

4. Was the tone of his or her voice aggressive? ____Yes ____No

5. Was the participant's anger level kept up during the exercise? ____Yes ____No

6. Did the participant exhibit any noticeable physical changes (mannerisms, agitation, tensing, and others)? ____Yes ____No

7. Was the individual unwilling to compromise? ____Yes ____No

8. Was the person's body stance aggressive? ____Yes ____No

9. Did the individual overreact to the situation? ____Yes ____No

10. Was the participant constantly disagreeable? ____Yes ____No

Role Play Checklist on Defusing Cues

The goal here is to find evidence of calming or defusing cues or self-talk.

1. Did the participant take deep breaths? ____Yes ____No

2. Was there evidence of self-talk to defuse the situation? ____Yes ____No

3. Was the participant talking slowly? ____Yes ____No

4. Did the participant refrain from jumping to conclusions? ____Yes ____No

5. Was there evidence that the participant was trying to control himself or herself? ____Yes ____No

6. Was the person calm? ____Yes ____No

7. Was the person listening to what was said by the other role player or players? ____Yes ____No

8. Was the participant trying to be reassuring to the other individual or individuals? ____Yes ____No

9. Was the person's body language nonthreatening? ____Yes ____No

10. Does the person's dialog make sense? ____Yes ____No

Role Play Activity on Hockey Revenge

Length of time: 15 minutes, including 2 to 5 minutes for the role play itself.

1. Event: You are on a local hockey team.

2. Number of Participants: four—two males: Fred and John (Number Ten), John Farren (your coach), and the referee, Hank Smith.

3. Situation: Johnny, Number Ten on the other team, has been taking cheap shots at you all night. One more time and you are going to get him. Their whole team plays dirty. You have taken all you are going to take—"thud." You are pushed and smashed into the boards from behind. That is it, even though you are not that big, you know you have a stick in your hand!

4. Ask for group suggestions for positive alternatives to defuse the situation.

5. Orally go through the Postrole Play Group Questions and Discussion Sheet (pages 46-48).

6. Go through the Role Play Checklist on Anger Detection (page 62).

7. Go through the Role Play Checklist on Defusing Cues (page 63).

Working Backwards Technique

Length of time: 10 minutes.

Purpose:

The main aim of this technique is to concentrate and focus the participant's thoughts on potential consequences of anger-related behaviors (such as aggression).

Sequence Structure:

A situation is given with an individual reaping the consequences of some angry outburst. This outburst may have minor or major implications. The resulting consequences are used to help reconstruct what might have happened in this situation. The group and the facilitator together try to isolate and find the initial incident that may have triggered the eventual consequences (there could be a number of incidents, a member of the group or the facilitator may choose one to explore). Fill out the Working Backwards Diagram Sheet (page 68) based on the diagram.

The accompanying diagram has two sets of boxes. On the left side of the page, Boxes One, Two, Three, and Four record the following:

Box Number One—	Initial incident
Box Number Two—	Behaviors leading to the initial incident that heighten or feed the individual's anger
Box Number Three—	Behaviors and self-talk the individual may have experienced before the resulting consequences
Box Number Four—	The consequences, which are given first, are written in this box (such as, a broken hand, losing a good friend over an argument).

Once the group and facilitator fill in Boxes One, Two, and Three, then their attention should turn to the right side of the diagram page. Here boxes are labeled A, B, C, and D. These boxes A, B, C, and D are directly opposite to Boxes One, Two, Three and Four.

These new boxes A, B, C and D represent spaces to write ideas that could have had a more calming influence to help defuse the situation. Self-talk, talking calmly, and modeling calmness are some of the techniques that could be used here. Box D also records the positive results that calming influences or self-talk can accomplish.

> **Goal:**
> Group members should be able to determine that there are alternatives and more than one way to deal with a situation.

Aggressive Behavior That Leads to Consequences	**Calming Influences or Self-Talk That Could Have Been Used**
Box Number One Incident—Jim and I were arguing about who the best baseball player is.	**Box A** Incident—It's only a discussion between friends—no big deal.
Box Number Two a. My voice became louder. b. I tried to outtalk him. c. I said, "You think you know it all."	**Box B** 1. Lower your voice—remember, you are talking to a friend. 2. Tell yourself, Jim has a right to talk. 3. Tell yourself, maybe I am right, but Jim is a friend—be careful now."
Box Number Three a. I pushed Jim. b. I pushed him harder. c. I saw red and struck out.	**Box C** 1. Step back, take a deep breath. 2. Allow Jim to give reasons for his view. 3. Give yourself a timeout. Tell Jim you'll see him later.
Box Number Four Consequences—John crouches over holding his hand. "It's broken," he thought. "Why did I hit Jim?"	**Box D** Positive Results—You did not hit Jim. Nobody gets hurt, and you and Jim remain friends.

Working Backwards Diagram Sheet

Aggressive Behavior That Leads to Consequences — **Calming Influences or Self-Talk That Could Have Been Used**

Aggressive Behavior That Leads to Consequences	Calming Influences or Self-Talk That Could Have Been Used
Box Number One Incident—	**Box A** Incident—
Box Number Two a. b. c.	**Box B** 1. 2. 3.
Box Number Three a. b. c.	**Box C** 1. 2. 3.
Box Number Four Consequences—	**Box D** Positive Results—

Working Backwards Question Sheet

Length of time: 10 minutes.

1. Was the scenario realistic?

2. If it was, why was it?

3. If not, what was missing?

4. What could be added to make it more convincing?

5. Suggest ways that the conflict may have been avoided (other than the example on the diagram).

6. Why are consequences so important?

7. Do you think that people always consider the consequences of their behavior when they are angry? Explain.

Sessions Six and Seven on "What Causes Anger?"

Target Group: Adult males and females

Time Allocation: Two sessions (60 to 75 minutes each)

Requirements: Chairs (tables optional) should be set in a small but workable "U" or semicircle shape. An additional small space should be used to conduct role play activities.

Performance Indicators: Each participant should know the following at the end of this module:
1. Two major causes for the causes of anger: "Outside" and "Inside" reasons
2. Better understand what "makes" an individual (including themselves) angry

Assessment Procedures:
1. Feedback from exercises and activities
2. Question and answer format

Methods:
1. Lecture
2. Role Plays
3. Question and answer sheets
4. Group discussion
5. Exercises to aid the participants' understanding of the subject matter

Training supplies, aids, and equipment:

1. Overhead projector (optional)
2. Transparencies (optional)
3. Camcorder and tape (optional)
4. Video cassette recorder (optional)
5. Flipchart pad and stand
6. Markers
7. Tape recorder and tape (optional)
8. Extra pens/pencils for group members
9. Handouts
   - Case Study Development Sheet (page 76)
   - Postrole Play Group Questions and Discussion Sheet (pages 46-48)
   - Role Play Checklist and Probing Questions (pages 53-55)
   - Role Play Checklist on Anger Detection (page 62)
   - Role Play Checklist on Defusing Cues (page 63)
   - Echo Dialog Question Sheet (page 79)
   - Working Backwards Diagram Sheet (page 68)
10. Sufficient copies of *Cage Your Rage* workbook to distribute one copy to each participant
11. Extension cord (if needed) (optional)
12. Extra bulb for projector (just in case) (optional)

Summary of Chapter 3: "What Causes Anger?"

This chapter centers around the causes of anger. Two main categories are suggested:

1. Outside Reasons—These are things outside or around a person that can make that individual feel angry.

2. Inside Reasons—These have to do with how a person feels or thinks and are subdivided into thinking reasons and feeling reasons.

How some person views or thinks about a situation often can dictate whether that person will choose to become angry. How one feels about a situation may create inner tension and allow that individual to become stressed out or shaken up over a variety of situations.

There are also doing or action reasons. These are the actual behaviors that an aggressive person may perform. Often, the way a person reacts influences what might happen. If a person backs off, a situation may be defused. If, however, a person chooses an aggressive and hostile stance, then the situation may become more volatile.

> The reasons that can contribute to influencing anger include:
>
> - Outside reasons
> - Inside reasons
> - Thinking reasons
> - Feeling reasons
> - Doing or action reasons

Equally important to note are the ways that can be used to help alleviate the aggressive behaviors that anger can produce.

Self-talk or running tapes can serve to help talk an individual into a situation or out of one. Does the person try to curb aggressive tendencies by telling himself or herself cues such as the following: "Be careful," "Don't be foolish," "This is not worth getting into a fight over." Productive self-talk can serve to help control anger and aggressive behavior. Self-talk also can be nonproductive and lead the individual into a pressure-cooker situation filled with frustration, tension, and agitation. The trick involved is for a person to talk to himself or herself, listen, use common sense, and wait, then choose whether to act. An individual may choose to back off and not instantly react in an angry, aggressive manner.

Chapter 3 (Session 6)

1. Review last session (lecture method with flipchart) (2 minutes).
2. Introduce today's session objectives and key points from *Cage Your Rage* (lecture method with flipchart) (5-10 minutes).
3. Warm-up activity: Ask the participants to describe people who they know who manage to keep their cool, even under intense conditions. Ask them to supply some specific examples (10 minutes).
4. Participants perform Role Play Activity on "Being Late" (page 74) (15 minutes).
5. Ask participants to complete the Role Play Checklist and Probing Questions (pages 53-55) (15 minutes).
6. Provide a break (10 minutes).
7. Facilitator reviews Case Study Development Sheet with participants (page 76). The facilitator, along with the participants, develops several case study profiles. After this is completed, the activity can be done for each case (15 minutes).
8. Participants complete the workbook entry in *Cage Your Rage* (pages 47-top of 52) (15 minutes). If they do not finish during this session, they should complete it by the next session.

Chapter 3 (Session 7)

1. Review last session (lecture method with flipchart) (2 minutes). The facilitator should check that pages 47-52 were completed.
2. Introduce today's session objectives and key points from *Cage Your Rage* (lecture method with flipchart) (5-10 minutes).
3. Warm-up activity: Use one die from a pair of dice. Ask a

participant to roll it. Whatever number comes up (such as "4"), the participant is asked to come up with (in this case) four possible outcomes for an explosive situation given by the facilitator or another participant. The individual has a time limit of 30 seconds to accomplish this. Repeat this activity several times with other participants (10 minutes).
4. Participants perform Role Play Activity on "Late to See Parole Officer" (page 75) (15 minutes).
5. Ask participants to go through the Postrole Play Group Questions and Discussion Sheet (pages 46-48).
6. Provide a break (10 minutes).
7. Review the Echo Dialog Exercise (pages 77-78) (3-5 minutes).
8. Ask two participants to do the Echo Dialog activity. Repeat with other participants, as time permits (1 minute each).
9. Participants should answer the Echo Dialog Question Sheet (page 79) (10 minutes).
10. Participants should do the workbook entry in *Cage Your Rage* (pages 52-53) (10 minutes).

Role Play Activity on Being Late

Length of time: 15 minutes, including 2 to 5 minutes for the role play itself.

1. Event: You are late for a date.

2. Number of Participants: one—yourself (role play may be suitable for either male or female participants).

3. Situation: You are half an hour late, and your date/spouse is not at the agreed upon restaurant. This person has always waited before when you were late. You need to discuss important issues. You ask yourself, "Why me, why always me?" A car drives by and splashes you.

4. Role Play Checklist and Probing Questions (pages 53-55).

5. Ask for group suggestions for positive alternatives to defuse the situation.

6. Participants should complete the Working Backwards Diagram Sheet (page 68).

Role Play Activity on Late to See Parole Officer.

Length of time: 15 minutes, including 2 to 5 minutes for the role play itself.

1. Event: You are on your way to see your parole officer.

2. Number of Participants: two—yourself and Mr. Jones, your parole officer.

3. Situation: You are late again. This will be the third time in the last four appointments. You arrive at the office; Mr. Jones does not look happy.
   "It's not my fault that I'm late," you say.
   "I've warned you before," Mr. Jones replies. "Punctuality is important. This is going in your file."
   You plead, "No, no, it won't happen again."
   This does nothing to change Mr. Jones' mind.
   You look at him with disgust and blare out, "Yeah, right, go on and do it. I'm sick of you anyway—just go to hell!"

4. Ask for group suggestions for positive alternatives to defuse the situation.

5. For other activities and exercises, review the Role Play Activity Sheet (pages 44-45).

It may be helpful to use one or more of the previously used worksheets either as a handout or on the overhead projector. The facilitator may wish to have a short discussion (5 to 10 minutes) on whether both males and females become angry over the same issues. The facilitator may ask: would they react differently—if so, how?

Case Study Development Sheet

Length of time: 15 to 20 minutes.

1. Uses: To help develop profiles of imaginary individuals with angry tendencies and aggressive behaviors. The profile's subjects should be adult males and females (use ideas from text, if needed).

   Profile:
   —Name (fictitious)
   —Gender
   —What is individual doing?
   —Brief description of individual

2. Identify anger triggers for this individual. Some examples:
   a. Verbal abuse—being called names or being put down
   b. Physical abuse—being shoved, pushed, or hit
   c. Easily frustrated—becomes very unhappy if things go wrong or pressure builds
   d. Negative self-talk—talking to yourself, things that help maintain anger or cause it to flourish and grow such as the following:

      - "I'll get him."
      - "He'll pay for that."
      - "She's always picking on me."

- "I'll settle this now."
- "Why me, why always me?"
- "I'll show them."
- "Enough is enough."

e. Embarrassment—A person agrees to buy four concert tickets—one for himself or herself and three others for some friends. He or she agrees to stand in the line to purchase the tickets. The group that is coming is fantastic, and the concert definitely will be sold out. Just as the individual approaches the ticket counter, he or she realizes the money for the tickets is home. "Oh no, how can I face my friends?"

f. Tension—the person becomes stressed out and allows tension to build

g. Can't take a joke—he or she is very serious and seldom finds the humor in things.

h. Believes that bad things always happen to "me"

i. The person dwells on one bad thing until the individual becomes upset

- List anger triggers for this case-study profile.
- List suggestions and ways this individual may reduce his or her anger.

Echo Dialog Exercise

Length of time: 15 minutes, including the exercise itself which takes 15 to 30 seconds and the question sheet. The exercise may be repeated.

Description of Exercise:

The echo dialog is a self-reflective technique that allows a participant to better focus on and understand what he or she is saying. This technique allows negative self-talk to be verbalized or spoken out loud. What an individual says to himself or herself effects how that person feels.

The dialog reflects an angry experience or episode where the individual is using self-talk in a negative, nonproductive way, which consequently reinforces the anger. The lead or main participant begins by saying various phrases and sentences to reflect that person's anger. The second participant repeats or echoes the words, tone, and intensity of the lead participant.

EXAMPLE

Participant Number One	Participant Number Two
That's it.	That's it.
I've had it.	I've had it.
He took my chair on purpose.	He took my chair on purpose.
He's always taking my things.	He's always taking my things.
Look. He's laughing at me.	Look. He's laughing at me.
Laugh, I'll give you something to laugh about.	Laugh, I'll give you something to laugh about.

Episode Ideas—The examples can be generated by group members, the facilitator, or participants may use examples from the exercises in the text itself. The dialog may be improvised.

Self-talk can help an individual avoid or resist angry feelings or confrontations. Or, self-talk can be used to plunge an individual deeper into an angry conflict or situation. It is this second variation of self-talk that this exercise aims to isolate. The short time suggested for the activity allows for and encourages a spontaneous burst of dialog.

A timeout may be needed if an individual participant becomes overly irritated during the activity.

Echo Dialog Question Sheet

First Participant:

1. How did you feel hearing your words echoed back to you?

2. Did you find your voice getting louder? When?

3. What could have been said by the second participant to make you feel better?

Second Participant:

4. Did you feel yourself becoming angry listening to the first participant and repeating the dialog?

Group Response:

5. What things could the first participant have done to step back from the situation?

6. (Ask each group member in turn) What one thing would you have said to try to calm the first participant?

Sessions Eight to Eleven on "How to Manage Your Anger"

Target Group: Adult males and females

Time Allocation: Two sessions (60 to 75 minutes each)

Requirements: Chairs (tables optional) should be set in a small but workable "U" or semicircle shape. An additional small space should be used to conduct role play activities.

Performance Indicators: Each participant should know the following at the end of this module:
 1. How to better manage his or her anger
 2. At least three techniques to deal with angry tendencies and behaviors
 3. That an individual can actively work toward better managing one's anger

Assessment Procedures:
 1. Feedback from exercises and activities
 2. Question and answer format

Methods:
 1. Lecture
 2. Role Plays
 3. Question and answer sheets
 4. Group discussion
 5. Exercises to aid the participants' understanding of the subject matter

Training supplies, aids, and equipment:

1. Overhead projector (optional)
2. Transparencies (optional)
3. Camcorder and tape (optional)
4. Video cassette recorder (optional)
5. Flipchart pad and stand
6. Markers
7. Tape recorder and tape (optional)
8. Extra pens/pencils for group members
9. Handouts
   - Role Play Development Sheet (page 43)
   - Postrole Play Group Questions and Discussion Sheet (pages 46-48)
   - Case Study Development Sheet (page 76)
   - Role Play Checklist on Anger Detection (page 62)
   - Role Play Checklist on Defusing Cues (page 63)
10. Sufficient copies of *Cage Your Rage* workbook to distribute one copy to each participant
11. Extension cord (if needed) (optional)
12. Extra bulb for projector (just in case) (optional)

Summary of Chapter 4: "How to Manage Your Anger"

Managing your anger is the controlling theme of this chapter. The last chapter highlighted the outside, inside, and doing or action reasons that may precipitate anger. In this section, techniques and ideas are given to help an individual better manage angry tendencies and aggressive behaviors.

This chapter suggests that by actively working on problem-solving abilities coupled with keeping one's frustration level low, anger can be managed. Lengthening one's fuse can make some situations more tolerable and less explosive. When a situation occurs, one's perceptions can serve to support a good experience with positive feelings or a bad experience with bad feelings. The ABC's of how emotions develop in a situation are important to isolate and understand.

A is for the Activating event or situation that arises in the outside world. B is for the Belief or self-talk about the situation. (Self-talk can aid or bring further desperation and frustration to the individual.) C represents the Consequences of one's actions or self-talk. The resulting action will resolve the situation or episode favorably or conclude it in a potentially aggressive manner.

> Relaxation is a technique to help lower frustration and tension levels.
>
> Aim to understand and recognize negative or self-defeating self-talk, and cultivate positive self-talk to reinforce your problem-solving abilities.
>
> Signposting anger helps the individual to read and recognize the warning signs that he or she may be becoming too tense, argumentative, and/or frustrated. Signposting acts as a thought-stopping procedure. In this way, an individual recognizes physical cues that he or she may be becoming too angry. The individual stops and attempts to counter this feeling with techniques such as self-talk and relaxation exercises. This offers the individual a chance to take a few deep breaths and allows the individual to employ some thought before taking a rash action.
>
> One method to defuse a situation is for one individual to communicate his or her feelings to the other person or persons. Avoid threats and calmly say that you are feeling angry but that you wish to work things out.

Calming others is a method, made up of six components, that can have a rational, settling effect on the other person or persons. The components include:

- Modeling calmness
- Encouraging talking
- Listening openly
- Showing understanding
- Reassuring the other person
- Helping the other person save face

Chapter 4 (Session 8)

1. Review the last session (lecture method with flipchart) (2 minutes). Check that participants made entries on pages 62-63 in *Cage Your Rage* workbook.
2. Introduce today's session objectives and key points from *Cage Your Rage* workbook (lecture method and flipchart) (5-10 minutes).
3. Warm-up activity: Ask participants to react to the following situation. You have loaned a friend $10 and a month has passed while the money has not been repaid. You need the money to attend an up-coming concert. You need the money NOW!!! You have asked your friend several times, and he keeps promising to pay you. How would you react? What would you do? What would you do if you found out that your friend was going to the concert? If possible, ask each participant to respond (7-10 minutes)
4. Participants perform the Role Play Activity "At the Party" (page 87) (15 minutes).
5. Ask participants to complete the Role Play Checklist on Defusing Cues (page 63) (15 minutes).
6. Provide a break (10 minutes).

7. Ask participants to complete Role Play Activity on "Out of Bounds" (page 87) (15 minutes).
8. Ask participants to complete Postrole Play Group Questions and Discussion Sheets (pages 46-48) (up to 15 minutes or whatever time allows).
9. Participants should complete the workbook entry in *Cage Your Rage* (pages 81-84) (10 minutes).

Chapter 4 (Session 9)

1. Review the last session (lecture method with flipchart) (2 minutes). Check that participants made entries on pages 62-63 in *Cage Your Rage* workbook.
2. Introduce today's session objectives and key points from *Cage Your Rage* workbook (lecture method and flipchart) (5-10 minutes).
3. Warm-up activity: The facilitator or a participant should describe a situation in which a person is upset and angry. Have each participant explain how she or he would intercede to calm down the person. Ask what he or she would say? How would the participant approach the person who was upset? How would the participant react if the person started swearing at them? Repeat this exercise with several individuals (7-10 minutes).
4. Participants perform Role Play Activity on "Being Cut Off" (page 88) (15 minutes).
5. Ask participants to go through the Role Play Checklist on Anger Detection (page 62) (10 minutes).
6. Provide a break (10 minutes).
7. Participants perform Role Play Activity on "Falling" (page 89) (15 minutes).
8. Ask participants to complete the Role Play Checklist on Defusing Cues (page 63) (up to 10 minutes or whatever time allows).

Chapter 4 (Session 10)

1. Review the last session (lecture method with flipchart) (2 minutes).
2. Introduce today's session objectives and key points from *Cage Your Rage* workbook (lecture method and flipchart) (5-10 minutes).
3. Warm-up activity: Facilitator or a participant should supply a situation in which he or she becomes angry while on a date. How would the participant act? What if they were previously in a good mood? In a bad mood? Repeat this activity with several participants (time permitting) (7-10 minutes).
4. Participants perform Role Play Activity on "A Spilled Drink" (page 89) (15 minutes).
5. Ask participants to discuss the Postrole Play Group Questions and Discussion Sheet (pages 46-48) (15 minutes).
6. Provide a break (10 minutes).
7. Facilitator should review the Role Reversal Outline (page 55). Participants should re-enact the Role Play on "A Spilled Drink," and follow up with a group discussion both comparing and contrasting the participants' dual roles (10 minutes).

Chapter 4 (Session 11)

1. Review the last session (lecture method with flipchart) (2 minutes).
2. Introduce today's session objectives and key points from *Cage Your Rage* workbook (lecture method and flipchart) (5-10 minutes).
3. Warm-up activity: Ask a participant how he or she would react if the participant were angry and someone tried to calm him or her down. What if it were a: a) stranger; b) close friend; c) girlfriend or boyfriend; d) spouse; e) person who was an adult that

he or she respected? What could someone say to calm down the participant? (7-10 minutes).
4. Participants perform Role Play Activity on The Restaurant (page 90) (10 minutes).
5. Ask participants to complete the Role Play Checklist on Anger Detection (page 62) (10 minutes).
6. Provide a break (10 minutes).
7. Ask participants to use the Case Study Development Sheet (page 76). The facilitator, along with the participants, may develop several case study profiles. After this is done, the activity may be completed for each case. (15-20 minutes).
8. Ask participants to read the "Afterword" in *Cage Your Rage* workbook.

> Any of the previously introduced handouts may be used after any of the role plays to lend variety to the activities and to reinforce previous skills learned.

Role Play Activity on At the Party

Length of time: 15 minutes, including 2 to 5 minutes for the role play itself.

1. Event: You are at a party with your boyfriend Tim.

2. Number of Participants: three—Sandra, Tim, and Lisa.

3. Situation: It has been a fun party with a lot of music and dancing. However, for the last forty-five minutes, Lisa (a friend of Sandra's) has been dancing with Tim (Sandra's boyfriend), and now she is getting a little too friendly. Sandra and everyone else at the party can tell that Lisa is flirting with Tim. Sandra cannot believe that Lisa would do this right in front of their friends, and she begins to smolder.

4. Ask for group suggestions for positive alternatives to defuse the situation.

5. For other activities and exercises, review the Role Play Activity Sheet (pages 44-45).

Role Play Activity on Out of Bounds

Length of time: 15 minutes, including 2 to 5 minutes for the role play itself.

1. Event: You bump a ball out of bounds in a volleyball game.

2. Number of Participants: three—you, Susan, and Janice (teammates). Additional participants could act as hecklers.

3. Situation: Your team is playing in an important volleyball match. You receive the ball and bump it off the wall. It was the

game and match point! You and your teammates are down. Susan and Janice blame you for losing the match. An argument breaks out.

4. Ask for group suggestions for positive alternatives to defuse the situation.

5. Ask the group to suggest ways this role play would differ if it were all males.

6. For other activities and exercises, review the Role Play Activity Sheet (pages 44-45).

Role Play Activity on Being Cut Off

Length of time: 15 minutes, including 2 to 5 minutes on the role play itself.

1. Event: You are driving home in busy rush-hour traffic.

2. Number of Participants: two—you and another driver.

3. Situation: One thing you really hate about living in the city is the rush-hour traffic. You try to keep your focus on your driving. You have not been feeling well, and things could be better at work. It's the end of the month and bills are coming due.

   Suddenly, a car in the next lane swerves in front of you. The car's blinker is not on. You almost hit the car next to you. Your blood begins to boil. You start swearing and decide to follow the car that cut you off. Eventually, the car takes an exit and pulls into a parking lot. You follow the car; you are ready to explode.

4. Ask for group suggestion for positive alternatives to defuse the situation.

Role Play Activity on Falling

Length of time: 15 minutes, including 2 to 5 minutes on the role play itself.

  1. Event: You slip on the ice and take a nasty fall

  2. Number of Participants: two—you and Tony, who is making fun of you

  3. Situation: You are running to the front door of your workplace to get to the parking lot. You slip on an object (or ice) and tumble backward and land on your back. You are hurt and slightly dazed. The parking lot is full of employees who are all laughing at you. Tony, a new staff member, is embarrassing you and being quite insulting.

  4. Ask for group suggestion for positive alternatives to defuse the situation.

Role Play Activity on A Spilled Drink

Length of time: 15 minutes, including 2 to 5 minutes on the role play itself.

  1. Event: Someone you do not know spills a soft drink over your jeans.

  2. Number of Participants: three—you, your date, and the person who spilled the soft drink

  3. Situation: You are at the movies with a date. While standing in

the concession line, the person in front of you turns and spills a soft drink over your jeans. These are your favorite jeans. This is your first date with this person. Your jeans are soaked.

4. Ask for group suggestions for positive alternatives to defuse the situation.

Role Play Activity on The Restaurant

Length of time: 15 minutes, including 2 to 5 minutes on the role play itself.

1. Event: You have stopped to eat at a restaurant before going to a party.

2. Number of Participants: two—you and the waiter/waitress

3. Situation: You are eating your soup and the waiter/waitress asks you if everything is all right. As you look up to answer him/her, you accidentally knock the spoon and bowl into your lap. You'll never make the party now. Your evening is ruined. Why did he/she have to bother you anyway?

4. Ask for group suggestions for positive alternatives to deal with the situation.

5. Participants complete the Case Study Development Sheet (page 76).

Session Twelve on "Afterword and Wrap-up"

Target Group: Adult males and females

Time Allocation: One session (60 to 75 minutes)

Requirements: Chairs (tables optional) should be set in a small but workable "U" or semicircle shape. An additional small space should be used to conduct role play activities.

Performance Indicators: Each participant should know the following at the end of this module:
1. That the skills they have learned will help change the way they deal with angry feelings and situations
2. That they must practice these skills to finally control anger

Assessment Procedures:
1. Feedback from exercises and activities
2. Question and answer format
3. Evaluation sheets

Methods:
1. Lecture
2. Question and answer sheets
3. Group discussion
4. Exercises to aid the participants' understanding of the subject matter

Training supplies, aids, and equipment:

1. Overhead projector (optional)
2. Transparencies (optional)
3. Camcorder and tape (optional)
4. Video cassette recorder (optional)
5. Flipchart pad and stand
6. Markers
7. Tape recorder and tape (optional)
8. Extra pens/pencils for group members
9. Handouts:
    - Anger Checklist #1 and #2 (pages 29-30)
    - Feedback Sheet (page 96)
10. Sufficient copies of *Cage Your Rage* workbook so that each participant has one
11. Extension cord (if needed) (optional)
12. Extra bulb for projector (optional)

The purpose of the Afterword is to get the participants to look back on what they have learned and to realize that they now have the skills to manage their anger. By understanding what anger is and examining their own patterns of anger, the participants now are more prepared for the challenges of living in today's world. For the participants, *Cage Your Rage* is a journal, and they are the writers. This means the book is an important part of their lives. *Cage Your Rage* is a good start toward feeling better, but the participants must practice their new skills if they are to reach their goal of controlling their anger.

Afterword (Session 12)

1. Facilitator provides an overview of the program's objectives and goals (use overhead projector or flipchart) (10-15 minutes).

2. Facilitator leads group discussions on Major Issues about anger (this page) (15-20 minutes).

3. Facilitator asks participants to retake the Anger Checklist questions for both #1 and #2 (pages 29-30) (7-10 minutes).

4. Facilitator hands back the first set of anger checklists that the participants completed at the beginning of the program. The participants then compare the present results with their previous results (10 minutes).

5. Provide a break (10 minutes).

6. The facilitator explains the Anger Diet (3-5 minutes).

7. Participants complete the Feedback Sheet (page 96) (10 minutes).

8. Facilitator completes the Evaluation Form on each participant (pages 99-101).

Participants verbally should acknowledge if they feel the program has helped them. Verbal feedback (yes or no) should suffice.

Major Issues

Discuss the following issues. You may want to have individuals respond to some of the questions in a written form.

a) Define anger.
b) How is anger good?
c) How is anger bad?
d) How do you deal with anger?

e) What situations tend to make you angry? What can you do about your anger in these situations?
f) What are outside reasons for anger?
g) What are inside reasons for anger?
h) What are thinking, feeling, or doing reasons for anger?
i) What is self talk? What is its importance for management of your anger?
j) How does relaxation fit into anger management for you?
k) How does a sense of humor help you in angry situations? How can you increase your sense of humor?
l) What is the relationship between feeling good about yourself and your anger?
m) Do you feel pleased and/or proud that you have completed this program?

The group may nominate the individual or individuals who have made the most progress since beginning the program. The instructor should emphasize that all individuals have made progress in this area.

Retake the Anger Checklist questions on both sheet one and two (pages 29-30).

The facilitator should hand back the first set of questions. Have program participants compare the two. Which answers changed? Have each individual identify the issues that need more work.

Administer the Feedback Sheet (page 96) (This sheet may be reproduced for use with this program).

Ask participants to submit their comments to the instructor who will relay them to the American Correctional Association (page 97).

Anger Diet Exercise

Exercise Name—The name "Anger Diet" is meant to be an upbeat creative use of jargon. Anger calories and control vitamins are also examples of this jargon. An individual desires to lose anger calories (aggressive, negative behavior) and increase control vitamins (calming, positive behavior).

Purpose of Exercise—Through this exercise, attention is focused on anger and aggressive, defeating behaviors as well as on positive, controlling ideas and techniques. This exercise process educates the participants about the dual nature of anger management. The theme is that anger management is susceptible to individual choice.

> Do the individuals wish to manage their anger wisely, or do they choose to allow their anger to manage them?

Facilitator's Goal—The facilitator should encourage the participant to cut back, curtail, or eliminate some harmful anger-related behaviors.

The results of the checklists should indicate to the participants the need to cut down on "anger calories" and increase "control vitamins." Remember, the goal of the "Anger Diet" is to help educate the participant about recognizing anger and managing it better.

Feedback Sheet

Comments About the Program:

_____

_____

_____

Positive Points Experienced From the Program:

_____

_____

_____

Suggestions to Improve the Program:

_____

_____

_____

Feedback to ACA

We are eager to get feedback from both facilitators and participants. Please tell participants that we are looking for additional examples for role plays or for examples of angry situations—other than what is in the book now. We also welcome illustrations.

Note: When you submit either written comments or illustrations, please include the following: "We give the American Correctional Association permission to use the enclosed material in subsequent revisions of *Cage Your Rage*." Include the individual's signed and printed name, the name of the facilitator, institution, address, and current date.

Send them to: Publications, ACA, 4380 Forbes Boulevard, Lanham, Maryland 20706-4322.

Suggested Readings

American Correctional Association and Police Executive Research Forum 1995. *Training in Cultural Differences For Law Enforcement/Juvenile Justice Practitioners*. Lanham, MD: American Correctional Association.

Cullen, Murray 1992. *Cage Your Rage*. Laurel, MD: American Correctional Association.

Cullen, Murray and Joan Wright 1996. *Cage Your Rage for Teens*. Lanham, MD: American Correctional Association.

Daley, D. C. and E. M. Read. *You've Got the Power: A Recovery Guide for Young People with Alcohol and Drug Problems*. 1993. Laurel, MD: American Correctional Association.

Davis, D. L. and L. H. Boster 1993. Cognitive-behavioral-expressive Interventions with Aggressive and Resistant Youth. *Residential Treatment for Children and Youth*. 10:4, 55-68.

Debono, E. 1987. *The CORT Thinking Program*. USA: SRA (A Division of MacMillan/McGraw-Hill School Publishing Company).

_____. 1991. *I Am Right, You Are Wrong*. Middlesex, England.: Penguin Books Ltd.

_____. 1993. *Serious Creativity*. Toronto, Canada.: Harper Collins Publishers Ltd.

_____. 1994. *Parallel Thinking*. Middlesex, England.: Penguin Books Ltd.

Glasser, W. 1985. *Control Theory*. New York: Harper & Row Publishers, Inc.

_____. 1988. *Using Reality Therapy*. New York: Harper & Row Publishers, Inc.

Harris, George. 1995. *Overcoming Resistance: Success in Counseling Men*. Laurel, MD: American Correctional Association.

Spielberger, C. D. 1988. *State-trait Anger Expression Inventory Professional Manual*. Odessa, FL: Psychological Assessment Resources.

Welo, B. 1995. *Life Beyond Loss: A Workbook for Incarcerated Men*. Laurel, MD: American Correctional Association

The "Working Backwards" idea used in this facilitator's manual was adapted from a problem-solving technique, which appeared in the following text: Connelly, R. D.; J. D. Martin; J. N. C. Sharp, *et al.* 1987. *Journeys in Math 8*. Gulf & Western Canada, Limited: Ginn and Company.

EVALUATION FORM on Each Participant

Participant's Name: _____ Date: _____

Name of Person Completing This Form _____

1. How often did he or she become angry during a typical week?

   _____
   1   2   3   4   5   6   7   8   9   10
   Very Often   Not Very Often

2. How often did he or she verbally threaten another person during an argument or angry episode?

   _____
   1   2   3   4   5   6   7   8   9   10
   Very Often   Not Very Often

3. Did he or she ever throw anything (such as a book or pencil) at someone during an argument?

   _____
   1   2   3   4   5   6   7   8   9   10
   Very Often   Not Very Often

4. Did he or she ever threaten anyone with a weapon (such as a stick, a chair, a knife, or a gun)?

   _____
   1   2   3   4   5   6   7   8   9   10
   Very Often   Not Very Often

5. Did he or she ever actually use a weapon (such as a stick, chair, knife, gun, or other item) to injure another person during an angry outburst?

```
   1    2    3    4    5    6    7    8    9    10
Very Often                                    Not Very Often
```

6. During an angry episode, would he or she continue to be aggressive verbally or physically, even when asked to stop by an others?

```
   1    2    3    4    5    6    7    8    9    10
Very Often                                    Not Very Often
```

7. Did he or she exhibit any verbal aggressiveness (swearing, shouting) toward friends, family, or partners?

```
   1    2    3    4    5    6    7    8    9    10
Very Often                                    Not Very Often
```

8. Did participant exhibit any physical aggressiveness (fist-shaking gestures, threatening with a weapon) toward others?

```
   1    2    3    4    5    6    7    8    9    10
Very Often                                    Not Very Often
```

9. Do you think the participant benefited from the program?

```
                1   2   3   4   5   6   7   8   9   10
No, not very much                                    Yes, a great deal
```

10. Does the participant seem to be getting along better with the others since taking the program?

```
                    1   2   3   4   5   6   7   8   9   10
No, not very much better                            Yes, a great deal better
```

About the Authors

Murray C. Cullen, author of *Cage Your Rage*, is a psychologist working for the Correctional Services of Canada. He is presently pursuing a Ph.D. degree in psychology at the University of New Brunswick under the direction of Michael T. Bradley, Ph.D. He is the author of several "hands-on" books on anger. His published writings also include material on sexual aggression and family violence. Present professional interests include polygraphy (lie detection), teaching emotional awareness, and work on enhancing participants' responsibility to treatment programming.

Ronald R. Cullen has been an educator in School District Number Eight in Saint John, New Brunswick, Canada for more than twenty years. Along with a Bachelor of Arts and Bachelor of Education, Cullen has a Master's Degree in Guidance. He has dealt with individuals not only in the classroom but as an organizer, volunteer, and coach in numerous sporting events. He was a recipient of a "Minister of Education's Innovation in Education" grant in 1994-95. Cullen is currently an instructor at Saint Rose School in Saint John, New Brunswick.